Miniature Goldendoodles

A Complete Guide to Caring for your Miniature Goldendoodle Including the Basics of Feeding, Grooming, and Taking Care of His Health

Josip Smith

TABLE OF CONTENTS

Introduction

Are you an aspiring dog owner? Then probably one of the most difficult and challenging parts of the process of deciding to own a dog is selecting the right breed. Note that you have plenty of choices, so you may find it quite challenging to decide on the specific dog who will enrich your life.

If you want a hybrid, one that you can easily pet and not necessarily a hunting dog, then the miniature Goldendoodle is certainly the perfect breed for you. A cross between the Poodle and Golden Retriever, you can expect this hybrid to have the excellent traits and features of the two.

This hybrid dog is also a favorite among pet owners because of its well-balanced and fantastic personality. Most Goldendoodles are famous for their intelligence, gentleness, friendliness, and affectionate nature. With that, they make great pets even if you have kids at home.

However, you can't just take home a miniature Goldendoodle without doing the necessary preparations. In that case, you should start by gathering all the important information that you can get about the miniature Goldendoodle.

It is where this book can help. This book aims to give you a comprehensive guide when it comes to owning a Goldendoodle – starting from the time you are still deciding on what to buy to the time when you already bring him home and take care of him until adulthood.

In this book, the new and tremendously attractive miniature Goldendoodle will be introduced to you. You will get to know some exciting facts about this breed that will surely help you all throughout your journey of owning one and making him a part of your life.

Let's start!

Chapter 1

Some Fun and Interesting Facts About the Miniature Goldendoodle

The miniature Goldendoodle is now a famous dog breed. It is a hybrid, a result of crossing the dog breeds, Poodle and Golden Retriever, allowing the Goldendoodle to inherit the most impressive behavioral and physical traits of the two. This breed also holds a positive reputation as a family-friendly pet.

If you are interested in taking care of one, then it would be best to start by familiarizing yourself with this breed. Some of the most fun and interesting facts about the miniature Goldendoodle that you have to be aware of are the following:

- **The miniature Goldendoodle is a relatively new breed** – It is a hybrid that first appeared during the mid-90s. It results from breeding a dog who has the coat and intelligence of the toy or miniature poodle and the gentleness and loyalty of the Golden Retriever.

- **The miniature Goldendoodle does not work as a watchdog** – This breed responds well to basic commands and training but you can't turn one into a watchdog. The reason is that they are not naturally protective of their owners even when in front of strangers or other dogs.

- **This breed is not aggressive when it comes to barking** – They do not even bark as frequently as the other dogs even if they get scratched or hear a squeaking sound. This trait is said to come from Golden Retrievers who do not bark as frequently, too.

- **This dog breed is like a tiny version of a teddy bear** – One can stand around fourteen to seventeen inches. A fully grown miniature Goldendoodle may also weigh around fifteen to thirty pounds. The average size and weight of this breed make them fantastic for smaller homes.

- **They come in three types** – During your search for a puppy, expect to discover around three variations of it – the American, the Australian, and the English breeds. The American miniature Goldendoodle often has a more golden shade while the English breed has bigger bones and a lighter color. The Australian breeds, on the other hand, seem to have the traits of Spaniels and Labradoodles who appeared in the earlier generations.

- **They have a fantastic lifespan** – Expect them to be with you for around ten to fifteen years.

- **The miniature Goldendoodle is available in various colors** – Among the most popular choices are white, red, pale cream, golden, particolored, chocolate, silver, off-white, black, and apricot.

- **They can inherit one of the three types of fur** – It could be wavy, curly, or straight. This will depend on the genes your chosen Goldendoodle acquired more. The manner of grooming will then depend on the kind of fur your pet has.

- **They are fond of the water** – They love to swim – be it in the swimming pool in your backyard or on the beach or lake. This makes them an even better companion during the summer, especially if you and your family love to go outdoors.

- **The miniature Goldendoodle is one of the brainiest dogs** – It could be because both the Goldendoodle and the Poodle rank high in terms of intelligence. This makes the cross between the two develop a high level of intelligence, too.

- **They are hypoallergenic** – It is mainly because of their Poodle-like fur that does not seem to shed that much.

By learning these exciting facts about the miniature Goldendoodle, you will be able to bring one home while being fully prepared for what to expect. Get to know more about what makes this breed a great addition to your home and how you can own and take care of one in the remaining chapters of this book.

Chapter 2

Top Reasons to Own a Miniature Goldendoodle

With the many good experiences shared by miniature Goldendoodle owners, it is safe to assume that this breed has a higher chance of giving you happy memories. This dog breed is a fantastic addition to your family's home – regardless of how small or large it is. You will surely love the extreme intelligence of this breed, making them much easier to train.

Aside from that, they are more than eager to please their masters, so you can rest assured of a convivial and jovial relationship with them. It also makes sense to own this breed that somehow resembles a tiny teddy bear if you have a small living space or have a couple of kids at home.

Why Should You Choose a Miniature Goldendoodle?

The following reasons why owning a miniature Goldendoodle is such a good idea may convince you to start shopping for one of its kind right after reading this book:

Natural playfulness

If you want a fun and playful breed, then you can't go wrong with a miniature Goldendoodle. This dog has a penchant for fun and play. He is energetic and fond of socializing and bonding with his owner.

You can even expect him to love outdoor activities, like long walks, hikes, and runs. With that, this breed is ideal for you if you are into outdoor adventures and you and your family are on the active side.

Friendly personality

Most miniature Goldendoodles also make great household pets because they are naturally friendly. Once you bring one home, expect him to be able to become friends pretty quickly and easily with other dog breeds, as well as cats and kids.

The fact that this dog does not bark that frequently is also a huge advantage, especially if you are someone who values peace and quiet. This breed has such a calm demeanor, which, unfortunately, does not make him an effective watchdog, but showcases his incredible friendliness and loyalty to his owner and those around him.

Highly intelligent

Another reason why owning a miniature Goldendoodle is such an incredible idea is that the breed is extremely smart. This dog is so smart that you may even think that he is human. Being highly intelligent, you can easily train your Goldendoodle to do a lot of things.

He can easily pick up whatever you train him, such as ringing the doorbell whenever he is outside. He can also quickly catch commands even when he is still a puppy. With that, you have an assurance that the entire training process, especially when he is still young, will go smoothly.

Minimal to zero shedding

The fact that the miniature Goldendoodle is not prone to shedding makes him hypoallergenic. Note that while dogs grow, it is possible for a type of protein coming from their urine and saliva to spread to their coat and skin.

The problem is that this protein can trigger allergies in many people. Those who are allergic to it may have negative reactions whenever they get exposed to the fur or hair shed by the dog. This is something that you do not have to worry about if you decide to take care of a miniature Goldendoodle. The reason is that this furry friend is hypoallergenic and non-shedding.

Not vulnerable to health issues and disorders

You will also love the vigor and stamina of the miniature Goldendoodle. The cross of two breeds that resulted in this hybrid makes them capable of fighting diseases. This means that the Labrador Retriever and Poodle's genetic diversity makes the Goldendoodle less vulnerable to developing a wide range of health issues and disorders.

They only rarely have signs of poor health. They are also naturally healthy that they have a lower chance of suffering from arthritis and hip dysplasia. It does not necessarily mean you have to be complacent, though. You should still get to his vet every now and then as he only has a lower chance of developing health conditions but is not completely immune to them. It is still advisable to have his health monitored from time to time.

Are There Drawbacks to Owning a Miniature Goldendoodle?

Most of those who have already taken care of a miniature Goldendoodle and brought one home as a pet agree that this breed is one of the best out there. However, before you finally decide to buy one and make him a household companion, you also have to take note of a couple of downsides.

That way, you can better decide if he is the right fit or determine the specific things that you can do to deal with the drawbacks of owning this breed. Among the drawbacks you have to watch out for are:

- **Requires plenty of exercises** – You need to give him a lot of activities every day, which may be a disadvantage if you have a hectic schedule. The need for a lot of exercises may also make the miniature Goldendoodle unsuitable for you, especially if you do not have enough energy and time to keep up with his active nature.

- **Prone to suffering from separation anxiety** – This dog may also be unsuitable for you if you can't be around with him most hours of the day. The reason is that he gets anxious when he is by himself no matter how you familiarize him with his environment.

Leaving him all alone for a long time may lead to separation anxiety, causing him to get bored and worried excessively.

This may even lead to destructive behaviors, like chewing everything he holds, vandalizing furniture, and shredding shoes.

- **Quite expensive** – We will delve deeper into how much this breed usually costs in the next chapter of this book. To give you an idea, buying a miniature Goldendoodle is not cheap. You may spend more than you initially expected considering his present popularity and good traits. It is all worth it, though, because of the positive attributes that this dog breed has.

Despite the mentioned drawbacks, it is still safe to say that the positive traits of the miniature Goldendoodle make them one of the friendliest and most fantastic dogs you can ever own. Most of them are gentle, kind, and sociable. They are also very attractive with their varying colors and coats.

If you plan to adopt this breed anytime soon, then your first stop should include the local shelter and adoption agency. You may also want to browse sites designed for new pet parents.

Aside from that, it would be best to look for registered and reputable breeders who can give you a wide range of choices for a miniature Goldendoodle. The next chapter of this book will give you a guide on purchasing this breed and the amount that you will most likely shell out for your new furry friend.

Chapter 3

Purchasing your First Miniature Goldendoodle: How Much Does It Cost and How to Pick the Right One?

If you have decided to push through with the miniature Goldendoodle ownership, then expect to have a wonderful experience ahead of you. Taking care of this dog may be challenging at times, especially at the beginning, but what you will experience once you become a parent of this amazing crossbreed will turn out to be fun, exciting, and rewarding in the end.

Be prepared to spend more than other dog breeds when you decide to go for the Goldendoodle as they are quite expensive. As a matter of fact, the cost of buying a miniature Goldendoodle is higher compared to when you buy a standard Golden Retriever or Poodle. It could be because they are among the most popular dog breeds out there.

How Much Does It Cost to Own the Miniature Goldendoodle?

Generally, you will spend around $1,500 to $2,500 to buy one. With the high purchase cost of this crossbreed, it is advisable to be one hundred percent sure that you are getting yours from a reliable and legitimate breeder.

Before you decide on a pup, it helps to visit and physically check him several times. Note that just a single visit will be insufficient in obtaining a general feel and sensation of his personality. One visit will not also be enough when deciding whether the dog is unusually fearful or aggressive.

If the puppy is completely healthy and seems to have a good personality, then the price is justifiable. If possible, choose a breeder or seller whose purchase price already comes with important services, like initial vaccination shots, some foods, deworming, blanket, and small toys. A reputable breeder also often provides a health warranty.

Note that you will spend approximately $300 in total at his veterinarian for four months with the veterinarian fees averaging $60 or so per visit. If your chosen puppy is not still microchipped, then the basic cost may increase by $50 as you will have to pay for such a service.

Moreover, you will also most likely spend $20 to $30 annually for the puppy's license. This cost will depend on the laws in your locality. Some locations also require the neutering or spaying of a dog upon reaching a specific age. You can get that service from affordable clinics. If you get it from a standard vet, then expect to be charged around $200 to $400. All in all, the initial amount you will have to pay that will most likely cover his first year can go up to $2,500.

If you want to reduce the price for getting your own miniature Goldendoodle, then consider adopting. In that case, you may only need to shell out $300 to $500 for the adoption fees. This will increase a bit, though, with the additional shots, medications, and neutering that your dog will need.

Also, remember that adoption is kind of challenging. Note that this breed is in demand nowadays, so finding a reliable adoption place may be more difficult than usual. You may want to try looking for a Goldendoodle Rescue to find out if there are available Goldendoodles that are suitable for adoption.

Moreover, check out the humane shelter or society within your locality. There are instances when previous owners of this breed decided to give their pets up due to certain reasons, like excessively high energy that they can't match up. It is a rare scenario, though, so you may encounter challenges when planning to go the adoption route. Also, be prepared to own a Goldendoodle who is already grown up when you adopt.

Factors that Affect the Price of the Miniature Goldendoodle

Note that even with the average price range of miniature Goldendoodles, various factors can still have an impact on its final cost. This means that the price of this dog varies from one provider to another.

Some factors that affect or constitute the purchase price are the following:

The reputation of the breeder

The reputation of your chosen breeder can influence the amount that you will be paying to bring home a Goldendoodle. For instance, some breeders make it a point to meet certain health testing requirements to ensure that the quality of their puppies stays top-notch. With that said, expect this breeder to make their dogs and puppies undergo a health test to ensure that their eyes, elbows, heart, patella, and hips are healthy and in good condition.

Choose a reputable and responsible breeder as much as possible. You may have to pay more than what you will most likely spend on pet stores, but it will assure you of great quality. Note that with the long lifespan of Goldendoodles, spanning around ten to fifteen years, you want to make sure that you are getting a truly healthy one from an experienced and trustworthy breeder.

Your chosen breeder should be professional, too. Looking for a professional one can assure you that you will receive the complete and authentic history of your chosen pet. A professional and legitimate breeder will also let you know about the medical conditions, vaccination details, and any other pertinent information you have to know about the dog.

It is not recommended to look for the cheapest breeder or buy extremely low-priced Goldendoodles from puppy mills as you may experience problems with their breeds later on.

Location

Another factor that may influence the cost of your miniature Goldendoodle is the geographical location. It can even affect the price by at least $500. As an example, miniature Goldendoodles located in California often cost higher than those found in the Midwest. If you want to save by getting lower-priced puppies from legitimate breeders in other locations, then make sure to consider how much it will cost to pick up or transport one. That way, you can determine if you can truly save from that approach.

Also, remember that buying from other locations may also be quite inconvenient since you will have a hard time touring the dog facilities. You may not also be able to inspect the dog's parents and see and examine your options physically.

Genetic type

When shopping for a miniature Goldendoodle, be aware that four major categories will differentiate the dog's genetic type. This specific genetic type is dependent on the exact percentage of species used and taken from the purebred parents with the goal of cross-breeding them.

Also, take note that each type starts with "F", signifying the word "filial", which is the generic term used for dog classifications. Each genetic type varies in terms of price. Here are they:

- **F1** – It refers to the mini Goldendoodle's first generation. In this generation, the crossbreeding process took place by using exactly fifty percent each of the parents – the Golden Retriever and miniature poodle.

- **F2** – This genetic type refers to a crossbreed puppy that results from the mating of two F1 Goldendoodles. Their genetics consist of fifty percent each from the poodle and Golden Retriever.

- **F3** – It is a result of breeding two F2 Goldendoodles.

- **F18** – It results from the mating of a purebred poodle and F1 Goldendoodle. The puppy that comes out of it has seventy-five percent poodle genes and twenty-five percent Golden Retriever genes.

The specific generation that your chosen miniature Goldendoodle belongs to has a major influence on the final price. The first generation (F1) is often the least expensive out of the mentioned generations. The succeeding generations require more work and breeding, which is why the puppies belonging to them cost higher than F1.

The coat color and type

The type and color of coat sported by your chosen Goldendoodle can also influence the final price. Keep in mind that this breed has different kinds of coat, including curly, wavy, and straight. In most cases, the type of coat can be linked to the Goldendoodle's generation.

It is also said that miniature Goldendoodles with curlier or wavier coats are a bit costlier compared to those who have straight coats. The main reason is that there is a huge demand for the curly and wavy coat considering the fact that this type is even more hypoallergenic and non-shedding.

Also, keep in mind that this breed has different coat colors that can cause variations on the final price. In this case, you can expect the cost to be affected by the rarity of the coat's color. For example, if you are eyeing a Goldendoodle who is multicolored, then expect the price to go up significantly than when you decide to buy one with a solid apricot or gold color.

If you are one of those who intend to invest in a certain multicolored miniature Goldendoodle, then it is highly likely that you will spend at least $1,000 more than your initial projection. This will also vary depending on where you decide to buy the dog.

Size

The cost of buying a Goldendoodle puppy will also be affected by his size. In the miniature Goldendoodle category, expect to find sizes classified as toy, teacup, and micro. One thing to take note of is that smaller sizes also tend to cost higher.

The reason is that it usually takes many generations of meticulous planning and breeding to develop a dog with the small size that most aspiring pet owners prefer. It is highly likely that the smaller ones can increase the overall purchase cost by as much as $1,500. As a matter of fact, some say that a multicolored teacup can go as high as $5,000.

Training

If you have the budget, then you can also go for Goldendoodle puppies who stay for a certain period with their sellers to undergo basic training before they are finally released for the new owners to take home. For instance, rather than taking home a puppy who is around eight weeks old and has not been potty trained yet, you have the option to go for an already potty-trained one who is around twelve to sixteen weeks old.

This puppy already underwent basic training, so expect him to know how to follow basic commands, such as stay, kennel, leash, come, sit, and potty. However, be prepared to shell out more money for such a puppy as this means that he already underwent formal training, making him costlier.

Supply and demand

At present, there is an increasingly high demand for the miniature Goldendoodle. It is the reason why its price is already high even if it just covers the basics. Also, keep in mind that reputable and legitimate breeders are those who will never force their adult dogs to produce more puppies. What they do, instead, is raise the price tag to cover the income they want to earn. With that, it is no longer surprising to see the hiking cost of a miniature Goldendoodle.

Package inclusions

The initial purchase price also varies depending on the package inclusions. If you only intend to purchase the miniature Goldendoodle, then expect to spend less than when you invest in a kit containing multiple services, like health checkups, initial dog foods and supplements, and vaccinations. The final purchase price will, therefore, vary depending on how many inclusions or accessories form part of the package.

Other Costs you Have to Prepare for

In addition to the purchase price of the miniature Goldendoodle, you also have to prepare for some additional expenses once you bring your puppy home and start taking care of him:

- **Healthcare** – Your miniature Goldendoodle, despite being naturally healthy, will need to be monitored or checked up by a vet occasionally. This is what you will have to include in your estimate for how much you will be spending for the pet once he is already at home.

  Generally, the healthcare expenses will range from $700 to $2,000 annually. These will include regular checkups, vaccinations, and surgeries whenever the need for them arises.

  An expensive health issue that this breed may encounter is hip dysplasia. If unfortunately, your Goldendoodle develops this condition, a surgical correction is necessary, which may cause you to spend more on his health.

- **Food** – You also need to consider how much you will most likely spend on dog food as it is his basic need. On average, those who own a miniature Goldendoodle spend around $500 or so every year on food. However, this cost will still differ depending on how small or big the dog is or how energetic he is.

- **Grooming** – One unique quality of a miniature Goldendoodle is he does not shed, which also means you need to have him groomed regularly. The grooming cost is usually $100 or so and it is often necessary to do it four times annually at the very least.

  With that, you may have to budget approximately $400 in total for this dog. His grooming routines may be expensive but the cost is worth it since it has several inclusions, like nail trimming, ear care, haircuts, and shampoo – among many others.

- **Training classes** – Do you plan to train your miniature Goldendoodle by enrolling him in a class? Then this may also add up to your expense. Find out how much do dog training classes in your locality cost. That way, you can dedicate a portion of your budget to it.

Aside from the ones mentioned, you may also have to spend on your Goldendoodle's supplies and accessories. Some of the things you will need to invest in even before you bring him home are a dog crate, dog bed, and other essential accessories, like a dog harness, collar, balls, and chew toys.

How to Find the Best Miniature Goldendoodle?

Undoubtedly, buying a miniature Goldendoodle and taking care of him can be quite costly. With that said, you have to make sure that you exercise due diligence and vigilance when shopping for one. That way, your investment will not go to waste. Your goal is to bring home a healthy puppy – one who will not cause a lot of problems once you begin caring for him.

The best thing that you can do, in that case, is to look for a trusted breeder. Look for one who has stable professional experience in this industry. Your chosen breeder should be trustworthy, legitimate, and professional. It is also important for him to have earned a great reputation when it comes to breeding not only miniature Goldendoodles but also other dog breeds.

You will know that your chosen breeder is a responsible and conscientious one if he offers the following:

- A genetic test, which is a big help in checking the pup for any inherited ailment

- Proper socialization, which should be done for puppies including training them to socialize with kids

- Reasonable and uninflated purchase price

- At least 2-year health guarantee

- Veterinary records that should also contain updated vaccinations and worming

Be extra wary when it comes to selecting the breeder you should trust. Keep in mind that anyone is capable of using a nice and enticing background when presenting puppy pictures and claim that the puppies they offer are naturally family-raised. They can make such a claim even if the puppies and dogs they breed do not leave their small kennels frequently.

To avoid dealing with an untrustworthy miniature Goldendoodle breeder, conduct extensive research about your options. One sign that you are dealing with a good one is if you continue receiving questions from them. They are as if examining you and your suitability to be the owner of the puppies they have bred. Other things that a breeder does that will show and indicate his reliability are:

- Raising breeds indoors starting from puppyhood – Good breeders also try to ensure that the puppies stay with their mothers until the time when they are ready to part.

- Giving you the opportunity to meet the parents of the puppies – The breeder will also let you take a look at the living area of the puppies.

- Conducting a test or examination on the breeding dogs to determine genetic conditions – The results should also be discussed with you.

- Providing relevant information about proper Goldendoodle puppy care, including grooming

– The breeder should also inform you about vaccination schedules and the temperament of the breed.

- Providing you with the puppy's health certificate – Such a certificate should come from a licensed and reputable veterinarian.

Also, be aware that certain warning signs should immediately drive you away from specific breeders. If you notice these red flags, then it would be best to begin your search for another breeder who is most likely to be able to provide you with the best miniature Goldendoodle that you can find:

- Have puppies who are not well-socialized, meaning they show fear when exposed to people they don't know

- Poor living conditions or very small cages for adults

- Does not provide health screenings

- No information regarding the living areas and conditions of the puppy

- Extremely low purchase prices for the miniature Goldendoodles

- Seems to pressure buyers to buy a puppy too quickly

- Lack of the necessary paperwork

Stay away from breeders who display any of the mentioned warning signs. Moreover, remember that even if a specific seller has a fancy and professional-looking website, there is still a chance that the puppies he sells online originated from puppy mills. Avoid them as much as possible as puppy mills tend to house dogs in extremely poor and cruel living conditions just to create puppies for money.

Such poor conditions may cause the dogs to become more vulnerable to developing genetic issues for reasons like careless breeding practices. You can likely save a significant amount of money when buying from such providers but you will be at risk of spending more on medical and veterinary bills because the dog you are getting may be unhealthy.

To stop yourself from buying from a puppy mill, never invest in one with the arrangement that your chosen puppy will just be shipped to you. It would still be best for you to visit the breeder personally and pick up your new furry friend on your own. That way, you also have a better chance of scrutinizing his living conditions and if he is indeed healthy.

Chapter 4

Preparing for your Miniature Goldendoodle's Arrival

Once you have finally chosen a miniature Goldendoodle puppy, it is time to prepare your home for his arrival. Note that while you will feel extremely excited about the prospect of finally having your pet at home, you should still remember that the entire transition may be too overwhelming for him.

Once you take him home, he will be in for a new and unfamiliar experience. He will be in a completely new world with people, sounds, and scents that are still unfamiliar to him. To ensure that the transition will be comfortable and smooth for him, as well as for you and the entire family, knowing exactly how to prepare for his arrival is a must.

The Shopping List

The first thing that you probably need to do when preparing your home for your new puppy is to create a shopping list. Note that he will most likely bring two toys, a training booklet, and a bag of dog food (around 3 pounds) once he will be taken over to you.

Despite that, there are still things that you need to invest in. Make sure to create a shopping list of the items he will need. Your shopping list should contain the following:

Dog leash, harness, and collar

Keep in mind that it is in the miniature Goldendoodle's nature to be extremely active. This means that he would want to have a lot of exercise time. In this case, you have to invest in a high-quality dog leash and collar, so you can take him out for a walk. It would also be best for you to have a harness around, especially if your puppy is one of those who are prone to pulling their leash too much.

When it comes to shopping for a leash, keep in mind that you have a couple of options in terms of its types. One of these is the traditional leash, which a lot of veterinarians recommend. The other choice is a retractable leash, which is not that advisable for Goldendoodles.

It is also important for the leash to have reflective threads, making your dog visible wherever he goes. You also need a handle, which is comfortable to hold on to, especially if you plan to take him for long walks.

If you intend to buy a harness, then it would be best to go for one with reflective trim. That way, you can let your dog use it even late at night or very early in the morning.

Crate

It is also advisable to invest in a good crate – one that your puppy can use for quite a long time. In most cases, Goldendoodle owners use a create in potty training. However, take note that it is not the sole purpose of the crate.

Once your pet gets older, the crate will also turn into a place where he can retreat every time he wants to sleep or gets too tired. You may also want to let him stay inside the crate every time you need to go out of the house and leave him alone. You can lock his crate for a while, so he will not be able to roam around the house and possibly destroy or damage something.

Once you begin shopping for a crate, it is advisable to find one that gives your Goldendoodle the chance to grow along with it. If possible, go for any of those that come built in with a divider. It is helpful as you just put this divider in the crate so your dog will be able to use it from puppyhood until he becomes an adult.

Bowls for food and water

It is also advisable to invest in high-quality bowls that your dog can use for food and water. Note that from the time your Goldendoodle reaches your home, he needs easy access to water and food and you can give him that with the help of the bowls.

The good news about these food and water bowls is that they are available in various sizes and shapes, so picking those you think are appropriate for your Goldendoodle to use is possible. You can even choose to invest in those that have water fountains integrated into them. That way, your puppy will get entertained every time he drinks water or eats his food.

Once you begin shopping for the bowls, you have to consider the eating style of your puppy, so you have to observe him for a while even if he is still at the breeder. A lot of Goldendoodle owners allow their pets to eat from a plastic Tupperware for several days until they became aware of the fact that their dogs constantly move their bowls around. You may also discover that your chosen pet tends to eat very quickly.

If you notice that the dog constantly moves his bowls around, then it is highly advisable to invest in one that has built-in rubber bottoms. With that specific feature, you will be able to let the bowl remain in its place. Also, if you discovered upon observation how your pet eats too fast, then it would be extremely helpful if you invest in a puzzle bowl.

Dog bed

A dog bed is also one of the miniature Goldendoodle puppy's essentials. He needs his own bed as it will give him a spot to relax and sleep. Go for a bed, which is large enough that your Goldendoodle can comfortably sleep on it.

Also, keep in mind that the Goldendoodle has the tendency to chew on the bed. With that in mind, look for a dog bed composed of sturdy and tough materials. However, the end result still needs to be quite soft that sleeping on it will be extremely comfortable for you. Make sure to get a bed that is made of tough material but is soft enough for them to want to sleep on.

One thing to note about dog beds is that they come with orthopedic versions. You should consider transitioning to this orthopedic dog bed once your miniature Goldendoodle starts aging. It is a great bed for him as it will be easy on his joints, making the aging process a lot easier for your dog.

Foods and treats

You also have to make sure that your home has plenty of foods that are suitable enough for your Goldendoodle's stomach and digestive system. It is also advisable to have some treats on standby. Make sure to go for dog foods guaranteed to help in making Goldendoodles happy and healthy all throughout their life.

In that case, it helps to spend quite a bit of time checking out all the ingredients used in dog foods. That way, you will be able to check its contents and some nutrition facts. It will help you determine which among the offered dog foods will let your dog eat and stick to a wholesome and balanced diet.

Also, ensure that the dog food you are offering is completely balanced in the sense that it can supply your puppy with all the essential minerals and vitamins he needs. A good choice for your miniature Goldendoodle puppy would be a puppy food designed for large breeds. The reason behind it is that this dog food is specialized enough that it can support the rapidly growing bones of your puppy.

As for the treats, make sure that they are small and soft plus easy to chew quickly. If possible, it should only be made using a single ingredient, such as a lamb liver. The treat should not also contain harmful ingredients, like BHA.

ID tag and microchip

You would never want your new miniature Goldendoodle to get lost all of a sudden, would you? With that said, it is advisable to invest in an ID tag and microchip. If you have an ID tag or microchip for your dog, then he can easily go back home whenever he goes out of the house and gets lost in the way.

It is possible to get an ID tag for your dog by either ordering it online or picking it up from a pet store near you. The good thing about dog tags at present is that they are available in various shapes and colors. You can, therefore, pick one that is a perfect match to his harness or collar.

As for the microchip, you can invest in one and have a vet implant it in your dog. You can also find those that you can do on your own at home. However, ensure that you are comfortable giving him a shot before choosing this route.

The best microchip is that which most universal microchip scanners can pick up. It can give you peace of mind knowing that an animal control officer or vet can easily find your pet using the chip and bring him back to you in case he accidentally gets lost.

Cleaning and grooming supplies

Make sure that you also have some grooming supplies prepared. One essential supply you should never forget investing in is a metal comb, which is essential for Goldendoodles with a curly coat. However, if your puppy has a wavy coat, then a grooming rake is more preferable. Both these combs can make your pet's undercoat tangle-free. You may also want to invest in a slicker brush, which is vital in fluffing his outer coat.

Other grooming supplies you may need are a dog toothbrush, preferably the finger toothbrush as you can easily use it when he is still a puppy, a cordless Dremel or nail clipper to trim his toenails, and a styptic powder, which you can use every time you cut his nail a bit too short. As for cleaning those unavoidable accidents, some of the things you may need would be Clorox wipes, paper towels, and carpet cleaner, including an odor or stain eliminator.

Toys

The life of your miniature Goldendoodle once you take him home will also become more fun and interesting if you invest in toys. Go for soft toys if he is still a puppy, but do not forget that he has sharp teeth that will make him chew on the toys fast eventually.

Invest in chew ropes as soon as he grows older as these toys are longer-lasting. You may also want to look into food dispensing toys as these items are effective in encouraging him to channel his energy productively. When shopping for toys, make sure to check the label and pick one that specifically indicates that it is non-toxic.

Ensure that all these items are around before you ever bring home the miniature Goldendoodle puppy you have chosen from the breeder.

Establish rules

Another important aspect linked to preparing your home to welcome the new part of your family is establishing rules. Note that your new puppy will most likely need a specific level of consistency right after he enters your home. The problem is he won't have any idea about the rules you have set in place, so it is crucial to decide on some things ahead.

Make sure that all the rules that you have set are clear. Inform your family members or anyone who is with you at home about these rules, so they can interact with the puppy more effectively. However, remember that even if it is crucial to inform the members of your household about the rules you intend to establish, it would still be better for only one or two members of the family to handle the majority of tasks linked to your puppy during the first few hours and days.

If you have kids, then they will most likely feel extremely excited to bond with and take care of the puppy but you have to avoid this as much as possible at first. The reason is that if you let too many people lead him and make him follow the rules, then he will find everything confusing.

Make him get familiar with the environment and the rules first before you let him socialize with every member of your family. That way, everyone, including your miniature Goldendoodle, will feel extremely comfortable.

Regarding the actual rules, here are the specific things you have to decide beforehand:

Bathroom location

It is crucial for you to decide on the bathroom location even before you welcome your new family home. Your chosen puppy may have already been potty-trained, but the fact that he is still unfamiliar with your yard and home may cause him to forget momentarily what he previously learned.

Also, factors like his nervousness, excitement, the ride in the car, and his urge to build a new territory, may cause him to want to relieve himself right after he reaches your home. With that, ensure that you have already set a suitable place at home or in your yard for his bathroom. Lead him this way upon arrival, so he will know right away what that spot is for.

A good bathroom location for your dog is that which is not close to where kids play. It also needs to be a spot, which is not that inconvenient for him to use whenever there is prolonged inclement weather. Considering that, the farthest corner of your yard, especially if it is too large, is not suitable for that.

Also, make sure that your chosen spot for his bathroom is large enough. He should be able to relieve himself comfortably many times without overlapping. If he finds that location convenient for the purpose, then expect him to relieve himself or go potty in that same spot. He just has to make a habit out of it and he will surely associate that spot with his potty.

Feeding location

You also have to look for the best spot for him to feed. You may think it is insignificant at first but you can actually enjoy several benefits from establishing a specific spot for his feeding. The usual recommendation is to feed him in his crate.

However, if you do not want to use his crate for feeding, then look for a spot at home, which will not interfere with your family's or household's usual traffic pattern. Remember that he will greatly appreciate it if he has a specific spot dedicated to eating and drinking. This is especially true during the first few hours and days he is with you as heavy foot traffic around his feeding area may cause him to panic and get too nervous.

However, pick a spot that you can conveniently and quickly access so you can give him water and food on a schedule. His food also needs to be stored out of his reach, though, you have to be able to access it easily. In this case, you may want to use a sealed dedicated storage tub or pantry closet.

After deciding on the location, make sure that it is only the area where he receives food and water, except, of course, for reward treats that you have to give whenever and wherever he shows and accomplishes good behavior. As much as possible, do not feed your miniature Goldendoodle puppy around your dining table or with fallen scraps on your floor. It will build the habit of him eating and drinking at the appropriate area dedicated to him.

A daily schedule

Most puppies are capable of developing good habits, especially during the first year of being with you. However, you can't expect your miniature

Goldendoodle puppy to form the right habits if you do not guide him well. With that in mind, another important aspect during the preparation that you have to focus on would be his daily schedule.

Before bringing him home, ensure that you have already set a schedule for him as to when he will eat, go to the bathroom, play, exercise, or do some other stuff. Being intelligent creatures, you can also expect your miniature Goldendoodle to be capable of adhering to the schedule laid out to him, so develop it in a way that is most convenient for you.

You also have to consider the schedule he is following from the place where you will be buying him. Find out if that schedule is also suitable for you. If it is, then you can just stick with it while familiarizing him with his new environment. If it is not so convenient for you, though, then you can create a schedule that you think will work for both of you.

Just make sure to dedicate a few days for him to transition to his new schedule gradually. That way, he will not experience a drastic and immediate change that may cause problems in his demeanor and overall health.

Once you have already set a schedule in place, ensure that your whole family is aware of it. Inform them about the schedule that they also have to stick to when taking care of and watching out for your puppy. By doing that, everyone will be on the same page when it comes to handling your new buddy, preventing him from getting too confused in his new environment.

Once you have finally established all these rules, it is highly likely that your Goldendoodle will have an easier time transitioning to and familiarizing himself with his new environment.

Preparing and Puppy-proofing your Home

Your preparation should also involve puppy-proofing your home. Note that upon bringing him home, your puppy will most likely be curious about everything that he sees in his new environment and surrounding.

Yes, he may already be trained to behave, but you can't expect him to learn all rules in your household, especially when it comes to what he can play with, so it would be best to prepare your home in a way that will be safe for him. Among the things you have to do to puppy-proof your home and yard are the following:

- **Remove everything that he may swallow accidentally** – Remember that puppies love to chew on different things, so ensure that most of the places he frequents are free of items that may cause choking when he accidentally swallows them.

- **Ensure that all electrical cords and cables are out of his way** – These dangerous cords and cables should be moved out of his reach to prevent accidents. If possible, tape them down to your floor molding or hide them somewhere that he can't see right away.

- **Take off all items that may cause injury** – Some of the items that may injure your puppy, therefore, you have to remove, are the strings of hanging curtain and some harmful objects, such as spare lumber.

- **Ensure that your fence is free of anything that may serve as his means to escape** – You have to closely examine your fence to prevent your Goldendoodle puppy from getting lost accidentally. There are times when the space between the ground and gate is large enough that a puppy can wiggle beneath and escape. Prevent that from happening by closely examining the living area and fixing whatever it is that may cause him to come out of the house without you knowing.

- **Do not leave harmful items on the floor** – Some examples are non-refrigerated foods and dangerous chemicals. This ensures that your pet will not ingest something that may cause him harm. Moreover, if you have plants, consider moving them out of his way, especially if they are prone to get knocked over. Transfer them to another convenient spot that will not interfere with your new puppy's daily routines.

Apart from that, look for something to block your puppy out of the way if there is a specific spot you do not want him to access. In that case, you may want to use a door but baby gates placed in stairways and hallways are also helpful. You can use these baby gates to prevent your pet from traveling over those points. Another advantage of doing so is that it will prevent the need to puppy proof all rooms in your house, which is not actually practical.

Giving your Entire Family a Heads-up

Everyone at home should also be aware of all the rules that you would like to be followed once your miniature Goldendoodle puppy arrives. With that in mind, you need to prepare them by letting them know about the rules your puppy has to follow as well as the proper ways to train him.

Do this even before your puppy's scheduled arrival. That way, they will also be able to form a consistent and structured environment that is convenient not only for the puppy but also for everyone.

If you have kids, then inform them that it would be best not to pick up the Goldendoodle and bring him around. You can let your kids hold him while sitting. However, you have to remember that puppies tend to squirm most of the time, so there is a high chance that he will get injured when being carried. Emphasize the need to be extra careful when carrying the pet to your kids to prevent accidents.

Also, remind everyone that most puppies will only feel at ease if they eat without needing to protect their foods. With that said, you should let your kids know how important it is to let him eat in peace by leaving him alone during mealtimes. If your kids bother your puppy whenever he is having a meal, then he will be prone to display defensive behaviors like nipping. Remind everyone about that so your kids and the puppy will be safe.

The First Night

His first night in your home may be the most challenging aspect of finally owning a Goldendoodle. However, there are some tips that can help you pacify the whole situation and make his first night easier for everyone:

- **Set a play session before bedtime** – Schedule a short playtime with him before he sleeps. He may feel tired at that time because he is still trying to familiarize himself with his new home, but it wouldn't hurt to bond with him through playtime. That way, he will become more familiar with you, which can increase his comfort level.

- **Do not let him eat or drink two hours before the scheduled bedtime** – By that time, you should be able to remove all water and food from his reach, so he won't be tempted to drink and eat too much that may only increase his need to get up several times at night to pee or poo. You may still have to take him to the bathroom at least once but it would be better to lessen the frequency by ensuring he does not overeat or drink too much water before bedtime.

Aside from that, expect your puppy to cry and whimper during the first night or so. Remember that it is normal. Eventually, he will get used to his new home. Try to spend a few days with him during the transition period, so you can also train him a bit until he becomes familiar with his new environment and finally forms new good habits.

Chapter 5

Crate and Potty Training

Now that you finally have your miniature Goldendoodle home, you can start training him. It would be best to have a training plan in place before you ever welcome the Goldendoodle so you can start doing it right away.

You have to train him on a lot of things, like behaving appropriately and socializing with other pets and people. With proper training, you can raise your miniature Goldendoodle into a well-mannered pet. Among the things that your training should focus on are the following:

- Crate and potty training

- Walking on a leash

- Not chewing on things

- Following simple commands, like sit and stay

- Socialization and behavioral training

The Basics of Crate Training

Crate training is one of the most important parts of transforming your miniature Goldendoodle into a well-mannered pet. One advantage of using a crate for house training your puppy is that it allows you to make him build that habit of staying clean. This means that he will never like the idea of sitting or lying in or next to his poop or urine.

Crate training is necessary for teaching your miniature Goldendoodle a lot of things – among which are discipline, obedience, and adherence to daily routines. Aside from that, effective crate training will encourage action and better communication between you and your Goldendoodle. It can also give you the freedom you need whenever necessary.

The first thing that you have to do to ensure that you will be doing this process correctly is to use the most appropriate crate for your miniature Goldendoodle. The biggest factor to consider when selecting the crate should be your budget. You also have to think about the present size of your chosen miniature Goldendoodle and how big he is going to grow within a certain timeframe. Go for a crate, which is not too small for him or he will outgrow it too soon.

One more thing that you have to do when it comes to shopping for a crate for him is to find one that lets both of you have your eyes on each other. By doing that, the crate training process will turn out to be smooth-sailing plus you can prevent your puppy from becoming too anxious.

If possible, invest in a crate training pad, too. It is necessary in giving your puppy the additional comfort and protection he needs. You have to make him feel less anxious and safe by choosing a crate, which is extremely comfortable for him. That way, there is a great chance for him to perceive it as his happy place all the time and not an area for confinement. He will feel at home and at peace with it, making it possible to transform it into his most comfortable part of the home.

Once you already have the crate in place, you can start the training. An important tip that will work for all miniature Goldendoodles regardless of their age is to address them by name prior to giving commands. Keep in mind that this breed consists of smart pets but you have to let them hear you call their names repeatedly, so they can start associating it with you directly speaking to and giving them commands.

Apply this tip to your Goldendoodle puppy, too. Even if you feel like you have already called his name excessively, you should still do it. If necessary, speak more loudly so you can emphasize his name even further before commanding him to do something. If you repeat his name several times, then it will motivate him to obey and take action.

Calling him by name is also good for him as he will feel like you are giving him your full attention. This is necessary considering the fact that affection and attention are among the things that a miniature Goldendoodle needs to establish a good relationship with his owner. Aside from that, these crate training tips may also be of great help to you:

- **Invest in the right crate** – It should be large enough that he can comfortably lie down, stand up, turn around, and move. If possible, invest in a large crate, which features a divider. It will let you provide him with a smaller crate while he is still a puppy then increase its size once he grows.

- **Make sure to give firm commands** – The commands should be firm enough that they are capable of engaging response from your miniature Goldendoodle. Also, make it a point to familiarize himself with certain commands by using words, like place, kennel, and crate. Whenever you command your puppy to go to a certain spot, make sure to point at it, so he will get the idea of where to go.

- **Feed him in the crate** – This tip is a huge help if you want to associate his crate or kennel with positive and good things, such as food. You can start feeding him in there so he can positively associate food with his crate. With that, you can train him to love his crate.

- **Offer rewards** – Make it a habit to reward him right after he enters his kennel or crate. When he is inside, close the crate's door then sit in a spot where he can see you. You should be next to him as much as possible during the time when he stays in the crate. Stay calm and do not stop giving him praises.

- **Release him after a few minutes** - Avoid confining him inside for too long especially if he is still new at the place. Do the process of putting him inside his crate for a few minutes while you are around so he will be able to retain the muscle memory associated with the repetitive actions.

- **Determine the toy he likes the most** – You should then use this well-liked toy to build a comfort zone for him. You just have to let him bring this toy inside so he will feel at ease and comfortable.

- **Increase the amount of time he stays in his crate slowly** – You can leave him in his kennel overnight but you should make it a point to take him out to have potty breaks when necessary. Just make sure to increase the length of time he spends in his crate slowly.

  If possible, do the increase daily. Begin with around five to ten minutes at a time then increase the time from there. It is much better to do it slowly instead of throwing your puppy straight into his crate for eight hours on his own.

- **Never associate the crate with punishment** – Note that your main objective for crate training is to make your miniature Goldendoodle go to his crate voluntarily. This is why you should never punish him by using the crate. If you do that, then he will not be able to enjoy his time inside the crate, making it more challenging for you to train him to stay in there at appropriate times.

However, when it comes to giving rewards during crate training, make it a point to avoid being too excessive. You should only offer the reward whenever he performs a good action so he will always have to look forward to it. Also, remember that in crate training, the rewards should be more meaningful and special. It should be something that will produce a memorable impact on him.

A wise tip is to schedule the crate training closer to mealtime – the time when he is getting hungry. It will produce better results, especially if he can already smell the fresh treat that you have in store for him. This should entice him to perform and engage, listening to your commands and following them. Do it repeatedly until he forms the habit of liking his crate. The secret is to avoid giving him the reward until he delivers and performs.

Once he gets accustomed to his crate, he will look at it as his safe space. He will wander around inside, relax, and use it to take a nap. Another advantage of training him into his crate is that it can make teething bearable and comfortable for both of you. Note that when your puppy is already at the teething stage, he will most likely chew on a lot of things.

You can use the crate to teach him to chew only on the toys and things inside his crate and only during the time when he is inside. With that, you also get the chance to inform him that chewing on other items at home, like your shoes and other personal stuff, is not okay.

Potty Training your Miniature Goldendoodle

The miniature Goldendoodle is undoubtedly one of the most adorable pets you can own. Despite that, you may still encounter challenges when it comes to taking care of this puppy breed – one of which is potty training. The reason is that potty training your miniature Goldendoodle puppy may take more work than usual. You have to exert an effort to take your puppy outside often and make him understand what he has to do when doing so.

The good news is that the eagerness of most miniature Goldendoodles to please their masters, combined with their high level of intelligence, may somehow make the entire process smoother. Still, remember that it may take a few weeks to months to succeed in potty training and this will depend on his personality and your consistency when training. In most cases, though, you can expect him to be completely potty trained once he is already six months old.

When it comes to potty training, remember that it is more beneficial to do it right after you bring your new pet home. Make sure that you have already dedicated a spot where he will eat and sleep instead of allowing your pet to roam the entire house. If you let him roam your home without dedicating specific spots for certain activities, then you will have a more difficult time potty training him. The reason is that it would be more challenging to monitor his activities.

Upon arriving at home, take him straight to the area you want to use for his toilet. Try to make him "go" in that spot. If he does, then do not forget to praise him. The goal here is to associate his potty in that spot by giving him a lot of praises the first time he gets into his new home. It can make him feel that it is worthwhile to save up some of his bodily functions to get praises and adorations from his new master in return.

Other potty-training tips that work well for miniature Goldendoodles are:

- **Set a consistent schedule for drinking and feeding** – It is also advisable to bring him outside right after his feeding and drinking schedule. Combine this scheduled feeding and drinking with room restrictions. This means restricting him to just one to two rooms. Teach him that it is not okay to sneak off to another room that is not dedicated for him just to control his elimination.

- **Take him out frequently** – This tip is extremely important when he is still new at your home. Take him out several times at the beginning of his stay at your home so you can train him that he has to eliminate at the right spot. As a guide, bring him out every thirty minutes to one hour every day. It is also advisable to take him outside as soon as he wakes up in the morning as well as after eating and napping.

- **Take advantage of some control words** - Make sure to use control words that he can easily associate with elimination. While he is going, make it a point to repeat the control words you are planning to use, like "go potty" or "go pee". That way, he can start following such commands.

- **Ensure that you bring him to the same spot each time you take him outside** – The reason is that such spot will have a lingering scent that will surely remind him of his previous business. With that, he can immediately identify the reason why you are taking him out, promoting ease in making him "go".

- **Accompany him until he does his business** – Make sure that you also stay outside while you are trying to make him eliminate or do his business. This will let you know whether he is successful. Do this until you have completely potty trained him, which signifies that it is safe to make him stay in the backyard to do his business on his own.

- **Offer rewards** – Do not forget to offer rewards every time he successfully eliminates outside. The rewards could be in the form of praise or treat. You can also reward him with a walk outdoors or some playtime.

- **Clap loudly once he is in the middle of eliminating** – It is a big help in distracting him whenever you catch him in the middle of doing the act even if he is not yet outside. It will distract him, causing him to stop what he is doing. With that, you will have some time to take him outside so he can finish his business and reinforce the habit of eliminating at the designated spot for it.

- **Never punish him for accidents indoors** – Such punishments will not be effective in teaching him the correct behavior. It may even trigger confusion and fear. That said, avoid reacting with anger or rubbing his face to punish him whenever there is an accident. The kind of fear that will be reinforced if you react with punishment may only result in your puppy doing submissive urination or elimination.

- **Use an enzymatic product when cleaning up accidents** – It is not highly recommended to use cleaners based on ammonia as those are incapable of completely eliminating the smell. The remaining smell may even stimulate your puppy to eliminate in that similar spot. You can use an enzymatic cleaner, instead, as it is more effective in getting rid of the odor. With that, your puppy will never go back to it and try to do his business outside.

When it comes to potty training, you should also try to manage your expectations. This means that you should not expect too much that your Goldendoodle puppy will immediately do his business each time you bring him outside. You can't expect that to happen right away especially if it is still the first time for you to introduce him to his new home.

As a puppy staying in a new environment, everything will be both exciting and confusing for him. With that, give him some time to familiarize himself with his surroundings. Be patient during the entire potty-training process, too. Remember that it usually takes a while for him to get the exact reason why his new owner brings him outside – and that is to do his business instead of exploring.

Chapter 6

Obedience, Behavior, and Socialization Training

Another aspect that you have to focus on once you bring home a miniature Goldendoodle should be obedience and behavioral training. The good thing about miniature Goldendoodles is that they are smart and eager to please, which somehow promotes ease when teaching him how to obey your commands.

Among the basic obedience commands that you can teach your miniature Goldendoodle are the following:

- **Come** – To familiarize your puppy with this command, it would be best to use a long leash. Just tug on this long leash while telling your puppy to "come". Do this a few times daily until he comes to you voluntarily every time you say the command word. This means he comes to you even if you no longer pull on the long leash.

- **Sit** – To teach him to sit, try pushing his butt down gently while saying the word. Make it a habit to teach him this command until he gets familiar with it.

- **Down** – Teach him this command once he already mastered "sit". What you can do is to entice him to lay down with the help of a treat while telling him the command "down".

- **Leave it** – This is a command that you can reinforce in your puppy by putting a treat in front of him while saying "leave it" whenever he tries to take it. Say the word "okay" if you finally want him to take the offered treat. Make it a point to praise him every time he follows such commands successfully. It is a big help in reinforcing the behavior.

- **Stay** – Another crucial command that you may want to reinforce to your miniature Goldendoodle is stay. You can teach him that by telling him to "stay" then walk away several feet from him. Monitor him. If he moves, then begin the training again. Reward him with praises and treats if you were able to make him stay successfully using the command word.

Aside from the basic commands, your miniature Goldendoodle's behavioral training should also involve taming him. This means disciplining him so you can get rid of any undesirable or unwanted behavior from his system as soon as they start showing up.

Note that your puppy can learn from you successfully if you reward his good behaviors and discipline undesirable ones. If he shows behaviors that are still nice and cute to look at during puppyhood, find out if the same behaviors are also appropriate and acceptable when he becomes an adult.

If you think some of the behaviors that he displays are inappropriate once he reaches adulthood, then you should curb them while he is still young. In this case, you have to be consistent as it can help him learn the most appropriate behaviors and get rid of the undesirable ones. All members of the family also have to apply similar commands and techniques to avoid confusion.

Another thing you have to remember when doing behavioral training is that the miniature Goldendoodle puppy will most likely associate a disciplinary action or reward with the displayed behavior within the past three seconds. This means that if you wait for more than three seconds to reprimand or reward him, then he will find it very confusing. With that said, you have to act on a particular behavior appropriately and in a timely manner.

As for undesirable behaviors, here are those you should consider correcting:

Biting/nipping

Your miniature Goldendoodle may display this behavior once he begins teething. In this case, you can expect him to have that constant desire to chew on things. Because it is caused by teething, you may have a difficult time stopping this undesirable behavior. Despite that, you can still try to correct it by directing him to chew on things and items that are acceptable until the time when he is no longer teething.

Also, take note that puppies only learn the basics of playing through biting, nipping, pulling, chasing, and wrestling with their littermates. Without his littermates, you and the people around your home will immediately turn into the littermates he is looking for. With that said, expect him to bite or nip you every now and then. When that happens, remove his teeth from the item he is biting or nipping right away. It could be your hands, clothes, or any other object at home.

After that, close his mouth firmly using your hand then deeply and firmly tell him "no", Make sure that your voice is also loud enough for him to hear. However, be prepared for him to do the same thing even if you already told him no. Do not feel disappointed and just continue training him if that happens. Do it until the time when he no longer nips, bites, and chews on unacceptable objects.

Growling

Your miniature Goldendoodle may also growl every now and then to relay if he dislikes something. It will not signify aggression at first. However, if you let this behavior go without disciplining it, then it may become an undesirable habit eventually. You should also avoid showing your fear every time he growls as he may learn that you tend to back down whenever he does it.

To avoid this behavior, you have to discourage growling actively. For instance, if he growls every time you come near his food bowl, then remove it right away and feed him from your hand. If he growls whenever you groom or brush him, let him know that it is unacceptable by continuing what you are doing despite his obvious resistance.

The goal here is to let him know that he is not the boss of the household. Everyone at home should also be trained in establishing the rule that your puppy is not the boss. This means you should stop them from feeling extremely timid and fearful especially when the dog growls.

You have to establish the masters in the household so you can train him to display good behaviors while he is still young. Keep in mind that if you wait too long to train him, then you may experience difficulties curbing his undesirable behaviors later on.

Jumping

Jumping is also another behavior that your miniature Goldendoodle may display. He may do it to catch your attention. While this behavior seems innocent and harmless at first, especially if he is still a puppy, you have to remember that it may cause danger once he becomes an adult. This is especially true if you are living with an elderly or some kids at home that may be knocked over by him when he jumps on them.

With that in mind, you have to train your dog in such a way that he can control his tendency to jump on anyone and anything. To do that, push him down then say the command word "off". Be firm when saying it every time he jumps on someone. Avoid rewarding him when he successfully gets down after you told him so, though. It is because it might enforce him to jump off first then get down after you say the command to get a reward.

Effective Obedience Training Methods

When trying to teach your miniature Goldendoodle to obey commands and correct his behaviors, remember that there are certain training methods that work. Keep in mind that all dogs have different preferences and temperaments. With that said, the most effective method of training for them differs from one dog to another. If you want to use the right approach, then you may seek the help of a certified dog trainer.

You may also discover that some dog training schools are keen on conducting interviews prior to the start of the actual obedience training. They do this so they can craft the most suitable training plan for the dog owner. In terms of training your miniature Goldendoodle, you will discover that his personality matters a lot. Your consistency and own personality also have a say in the results of the training.

If your goal is to train him using methods that focus on positive associations and reinforcements, then the following will surely work for the both of you:

- **Clicker training** – This training method is one of the most popular approaches used by certified dog trainers. It requires you to use a handheld device, which works by producing a clicking sound. Every time you need to give your puppy a reward as a positive reinforcement for obeying your commands, the toy, praise, or treat you are offering him should be accompanied by the clicking sound.

Eventually, he can associate the sound produced by the clicker with a reward. You can use this method until you notice that your dog has become more reliable when it comes to obeying commands.

In that case, you can start giving the rewards only occasionally. Even with the reduced rewards, you should still continue using the clicker. The reason is that it usually serves as an indicator that you are praising him for his good behaviors.

- **Food reward** – You can also train your miniature Goldendoodle to be more obedient by offering foods as rewards. In this case, you have to find out first the specific foods that are sure to motivate him. You may offer a traditional dog treat every time he performs as he is told.

  You can also offer less traditional foods as treats, including some pieces of cheese, baby carrots, bits of hotdog, and cold cuts. The goal here is to elicit specific behaviors in him by retaining his attention. You can achieve that through foods whenever he does something that pleases you during the obedience training.

- **Toy reward** – You will also highly likely succeed in your obedience training if you offer toys as rewards for your dog. A toy is a great alternative if you notice that he intends to choose toys over other treats and rewards. You can also offer this reward in the form of sufficient playtime. It is useful for more specialized training.

- **Praise reward** – Another way to train your miniature Goldendoodle to be more obedient and establish good behaviors is to reward him with praises. It works well for this breed considering the fact that the miniature Goldendoodle is so people-oriented. This breed is often attuned with humans and wants to please their masters.

  In most cases, you can use praises together with clicker training and food or toy rewards. You can also occasionally integrate attention and praises on their own when teaching your pet obedience commands. The good thing about offering praises is that it can significantly improve his trust in you as well as his self-confidence.

Socialization Training

It is also advisable to socialize your miniature Goldendoodle as early as possible. Note that socialization training is always a vital component of the process of caring for this dog breed. Begin this training when he is still around eight weeks old.

You may want to follow what other dog owners did when it comes to socializing their puppies – and that is by enrolling them in puppy classes. In that case, you can also introduce him to other puppies, which is a great way to improve his socialization skills.

The good thing about puppy classes is that they can also help your puppy learn about basic commands, like sitting and staying. The classes will also teach him the basics of walking on a leash.

Aside from introducing your miniature Goldendoodle to other puppies, it is also advisable to expose him to different kinds of environments and sounds. Do this during his first few months. Give him the opportunity to experience various social environments, too.

These should include not only other dogs but also people. This is important to prevent him from displaying fear and anxiety whenever he faces situations involving new animals and people.

Once you start the socialization training, make it a point to think of and consider all those situations he may encounter in the future.

Keep in mind that your primary goal for this training is to make him feel relaxed whenever he is around new pets, people, cars, vets, large crowds, and any other objects that may otherwise cause him to be anxious like stairs and honking horns.

You have to make him get used to such environments and situations. He should be able to build new experiences, meet new animals and people, and learn new behaviors comfortably at around two to four months.

When introducing him to new people and environments, be aware that he may feel scared and anxious at first. In that case, give him positive reinforcements for every appropriate behavior displayed.

Make it a point to show your support to him whenever he displays fear, too. That way, he will become more familiar with almost everything that you expose him to, preventing him from behaving undesirably.

With proper socialization training, you can expect your miniature Goldendoodle to adapt easily to new animals, people, and environments at four months and above. It is also the key to preventing difficulties when doing the obedience training since he is already familiar with almost everything that is happening around him.

Chapter 7

The Miniature Goldendoodle Diet: What Should you Feed your Pet?

Now, let us talk about another interesting topic associated with taking care of a miniature Goldendoodle – that is his diet. The question is what can you feed your puppy as soon as he gets at home? What nutrients does he need? And what adjustments do you have to make regarding his diet and feeding as soon as he grows older? Let's find out the answers to that question in this specific chapter.

What to Feed your Miniature Goldendoodle Based on Age?

When it comes to determining the specific foods that meet the needs of your miniature Goldendoodle, his age matters a lot. It also helps determine the feeding quantity he needs along with other factors like his actual size, basal metabolism rate, and activity level. If he is extremely active, then you also have to provide him with more foods. Basically, here is a rough guide on what to feed your new pet depending on his age:

- **6 weeks** – If you have a 6-week-old miniature Goldendoodle, then you can classify him as a baby. With that in mind, he still needs the support of his mother to get the nutrients his body needs for growth and development. At this stage, it would be best for the puppy to feed freely from his mother. The reason is that his mother produces all the nutrients and other good stuff he needs for survival.

- **10 weeks** – Once he reaches ten weeks, you can wean him off his mother's milk. This is also the right time to begin introducing delicious puppy foods into his everyday feedings. Note that this will involve a transition from a liquid to a solid diet, so it would be ideal to try softening or smoothening the change with the help of wet canned choices. They serve as excellent transitional foods.

By using these foods, the sensitive stomach of your puppy will not be drastically affected, making it possible for him to familiarize himself comfortably with the new foods introduced to him. It is also helpful in ensuring that he will have healthier stools, preventing him from causing a mess that you have to clean afterward.

- **12 weeks** – During this time, your miniature Goldendoodle can start taking the transition from wet foods into dry kibbles. In case you were successful in weaning him in the past, it would be much better to apply a similar gentle approach, thereby ensuring that his digestive system will be able to adjust slowly to the new foods being introduced to him.

One more thing you should keep in mind is that dry foods have less water. With that in mind, do not forget to set aside some water for your puppy, so he can always easily access it every time he needs to drink. It is also crucial in keeping him fully hydrated.

- **3 months** – As soon as he hit the 3-month-old mark, your miniature Goldendoodle has most likely completed his transition from wet to dry foods. In this case, it is surely the perfect time for you to check out the labels of the foods you are feeding him. That way, you can pick a food or recipe that is perfect for his specific life stage.

  What you should look for during this age is a dog food labeled as puppy formula. It is suitable for the needs of a 3-month-old miniature Goldendoodle since it is specifically designed to contain the nutrients needed by his growing and developing body. Keep in mind that foods labeled as adult life stage have a different formulation. It does not also provide adequate support for the additional calories needed for his growth.

- **5 months** – Upon reaching five months, it is crucial to make your miniature Goldendoodle stick to dry foods. This is also the time when you can lessen the frequency of his feedings. Two meals daily are even enough for his age. Avoid leaving foods that he can munch on during this stage as it may only cause him to overeat and gain excess weight.

- **1 year** – This is the time when your miniature Goldendoodle has already matured. It means that he has reached adulthood, which also indicates that his eating frequency also gets lower. There are even instances when there are leftovers from the foods you feed him. In case you notice that, then maybe it would be a good idea to reduce the kibbles you feed him during each meal.

Nutritional Requirements

To ensure that you are choosing the right foods for your miniature Goldendoodle, you have to learn about this dog's specific nutritional requirements. Note that your new pet will only grow and develop the best and the healthiest way by feeding him with foods that can supply his body with all the nutrients it needs.

Basically, he needs the following nutrients to ensure that he grows into a healthy and active dog:

Protein

Just like other dogs, your miniature Goldendoodle needs a good supply of protein. It is, therefore, the main requirement in his meals. The good news is that your pet can gain protein from various sources – among which are whole meats, like beef, fish, and buffalo.

Another source of protein is a plant-based food. You just have to make sure that the plants you have chosen for him to eat are easy for his stomach and digestive system to process.

Also, remember that animal protein should always be his main source of protein. Make it a point to choose formulas specifically made and designed for the life stage of a puppy. The reason is that its protein to carb and fat ratio is usually perfect for a growing and developing dog.

Fiber

It is also crucial for your miniature Goldendoodle's diet to have enough fiber. This nutrient is vital for him for a couple of reasons – one of which is that your puppy will most likely have a lot of energy through it. Aside from that, fiber ensures that your dog will have a healthy and smoothly functioning digestive tract.

Fiber can, therefore, ensure that your new buddy will not deal with a stomachache. It can also prevent him from experiencing problems when passing food. By making foods rich in fiber a part of his daily diet, you can help make his digestion work properly, thereby preventing possible issues on his health.

Fats and fatty acids

Healthy fats and fatty acids are also among the nutrients needed by your puppy. These are helpful in ensuring that his eyes and brain develop in a healthy manner. You can supply his body with fatty acids, particularly Omega 3 and Omega 6, by including their supplement variations in your dog's dry foods.

The good thing about including fats in his diet is that it can help him have consistently high energy. This will let him play, take a long walk with you, run, and explore. Some of the excellent sources of healthy fats that are good for your dog are oils and flaxseed. You can also let him eat chicken fat, but make sure that he does not have any allergic reaction to it first.

As for the fatty acids, like the Omegas, you can expect them to play a major role in improving the shine, health, and look of your miniature Goldendoodle's skin and coat. It can improve his look, particularly in his eyes, coat, and weight, which can also signify that he is physically healthy.

Carbohydrates

The diet of your miniature Goldendoodle should also consist of foods rich in carbs. Note that carbohydrates form a vital part of his dietary requirements. He needs this nutrient to ensure that his level of blood sugar remains stable. However, you have to exercise caution when it comes to adding carbs into his diet. The reason is that you have to avoid going extremely beyond what he needs.

Keep in mind that excessive carb intake may also cause his blood sugar to spike suddenly, so minimize it as much as possible. If you are already feeding him with high-quality dog food specifically formulated for the life stages of puppies or adults, then the carb content is most likely okay. Just make sure to adhere to the feeding instructions indicated in the label to avoid going beyond what he needs.

Essential vitamins, antioxidants, and minerals

It is also important to serve your miniature Goldendoodle with foods that supply his body with all the essential vitamins, antioxidants, and minerals he needs. Fortunately, you can now find several high-quality dog foods containing supplementary minerals and vitamins capable of supporting the health of canines.

Your dog needs these vitamins and minerals to ensure the proper growth and development of his organs and tissues. He also needs these nutrients throughout his entire lifespan. Aside from that, all these nutrients contain long-lasting properties designed to fight the negative effects of aging on your dog.

By properly nourishing his body, he can prevent himself from acquiring certain diseases. Furthermore, most top-quality dog foods contain antioxidants that can fight the harmful effects of free radicals on his body.

Water

In addition to all the nutrients mentioned, you have to make sure that your miniature Goldendoodle can also easily access water. It is necessary unless his vet suggests withholding water from him. He should be able to access water easily as he would love to take a drink, especially after a long walk.

It is also vital to keep him hydrated. By ensuring that your dog stays hydrated, you have an assurance that all the nutrients present in all the foods he is taking in will be moved to various parts and cells of his body.

Note that bodily functions depend on your dog's hydration level, so ensure that there is a good supply of it to quench his thirst. However, if you are still in the stage of housetraining him, then you may want to remove his bowl of water overnight. Just give it to him during the day.

Recommended Foods

The best foods you can offer to your dog will always depend on your preferences, though, you have to consider factors, like your budget, food availability, the current health profile of your pet, and his age. Some vouch for the goodness of wet and dry commercial dog foods.

However, there are also those who say that the best diet plan for miniature Goldendoodles when they are still puppies is one with medium-calorie content and quite low-protein content. The protein should not exceed around 25%.

A lot of breeders also agree on the goodness of a raw food diet not only for puppies but also for adults and adolescents. However, it is crucial to vary the fiber, fat, and protein contents for every stage to ensure that your dog receives the exact nutrients he needs.

When it comes to feeding your miniature Goldendoodle, be aware that you have a couple of options – commercial dog foods and homemade ones (the ones you personally make at home).

Commercial Dog Foods

A lot of dog owners choose commercial products because these promote ease in ensuring that their pets eat a balanced diet. Commercial dog foods do not also take too much time to prepare. When searching for a high-quality one, go for a product, which has a good source of protein as its main ingredient.

Your best option probably is the dry dog kibble. It is a dry food, which is easy to store and feed. Aside from that, it is beneficial for his teeth. The reason is that every time he bites on his dry dog kibble, it tends to knock off some of the tartar that has developed on his teeth.

Homemade Dog Foods

You can also choose to feed your miniature Goldendoodle with homemade and human foods. Just remember that some of these dogs have sensitive stomachs, which means you have to be extra careful when it comes to serving them homemade foods. You can cook food for him, especially if you are not fond of giving him commercial products. Ensure that the foods you cook for him can meet his dietary and nutritional requirements.

If you decide to choose this approach, then you will be pleased to know that you can now access a lot of sites that provide recipes designed for miniature Goldendoodles. Among the foods and ingredients that you can prepare guaranteed to provide your Goldendoodle with a lot of nutrients plus promote ease of digestion are:

- Lamb, beef, chicken, and other sources of white meat for protein

- Vegetables, like asparagus, broccoli, cabbage, bell peppers, cauliflower, carrots, and Brussels sprouts

- Fruits, like apples that are ideal for senior Goldendoodles who have low metabolic rate – Ensure that the apples no longer have seeds upon serving. Other fruits that miniature Goldendoodles love are bananas, apricots, cantaloupe, blueberries, and blackberries.

Make it a point to include the mentioned foods, fruits, and veggies in the homemade diet of your miniature Goldendoodle. It is also possible for you to serve these foods as treats or rewards.

Foods to Avoid

You also have to know some of the foods that are dangerous to your miniature Goldendoodle. That way, you will not make the mistake of feeding these items to him and causing problems with his health. Among the foods that are unsafe to feed to this dog breed are:

- Prunes

- Raisins or grapes

- Large amounts of dairy – It is not good for his digestive system as it is not ideal for processing dairy. You can still let him eat dairy products but keep it to a minimum.

- Citrus fruits – not recommended as they often trigger an upset stomach

- Coffee

- Garlic and onions

- Avocado

- Chocolate, especially baker's and dark chocolates as they are extremely toxic to dogs

- Salty foods

- Macadamia nuts

- Foods rich in artificial sugar

- Cherries as they are toxic not only to dogs but also to cats

- Soda

- Undercooked and raw meat and eggs

Make sure that you also inform the people in your household about these prohibited foods, so they will not make the mistake of feeding your dog with them.

How Much and How Often Should You Feed your Miniature Goldendoodle?

In most cases, you can follow the feeding guidelines often indicated at the back of commercial dog food bags. There are also instances when you have to increase the recommended amount of food a bit, especially if you notice that he is the extremely active type.

As a guide, though, you can stick to the one cup of dog food for every fifteen pounds of weight daily. This means that if your dog weighs around 30 pounds, then you should give him a total of two cups of food every day. You can divide it into one cup two times daily.

It is also crucial for you to keep track of his weight, so you will know right away if the amount of food you are feeding him is enough. If he seems too thin for his age, then it would be best to increase his servings. If he begins gaining extra weight, then reduce the amount of food you serve.

Consider his exercises and activities, too. Note that there are miniature Goldendoodles who also take part in sports and agility training. If he is on his competition and training months, then you have to increase his food consumption. That way, he can have the additional energy he needs for this season. After that season, though, you have to reduce his food intake to ensure that his weight remains at a healthy level.

As for the frequency of feeding, it should be around twice to thrice daily. Ensure that what you feed him makes him feel full, so he will not display behaviors linked to food aggressions. With that, you can lower the risk of him destroying some items at home or eating those he should not eat.

Dealing with a Picky Eater

Is your miniature Goldendoodle picky with his foods? Then you don't have to worry too much as there are ways to deal with it. Here are some simple tips that you can use to encourage him to eat whatever it is you are serving him:

- **Add a bit of warm water to his food** – By adding water, especially to dry kibbles, you can create a gravy-like consistency that he may love. It can also soften the kibble, which can make it easier for him to eat.

- **Mix in a bit of canned food** – Putting in a bit of canned food to his dry food can make the mixture more enticing to him. A small spoonful of it mixed with his usual dry foods is often enough. Mix them well. The reason is that if you do not mix the wet and dry foods well, then your dog will be at risk of only eating the wet part on top. He will then leave the remaining dry kibble beneath it.

- **Change his diet** – You may also want to change his main source of protein. Remember that your miniature Goldendoodle may start becoming picky because he does not like something about his diet. For instance, if his main diet consists of rice and chicken and you feel like he does not enjoy it, then you may want to change it into rice and lamb. You can also switch it to duck protein.

It also helps to consult a veterinarian especially if your dog stops eating his food all of a sudden. It could be that he has developed an illness that is ruining his appetite. A good vet can scrutinize the present condition of your Goldendoodle, giving you information about whether or not something is causing his loss of appetite.

Chapter 8

How to Take Care of His Health?

You and your miniature Goldendoodle will surely have the best time of your lives together if both of you are healthy. This means that you have to stay committed to help him have the best health if you want to be his master. In that case, you have to be aware of several areas of his health that you have to focus on when planning to take care of this breed.

Vaccinations and Vet Visits

One of the most important things that you have to do once you become a fur parent is to ensure that your pet receives proper and timely vaccinations. This means that right after you receive your miniature Goldendoodle, you should prioritize setting an appointment with your chosen veterinarian.

This is an important step as the veterinarian will spend time examining the present health of your puppy. It will also be the time when the previous vaccines he received will be reviewed. During your vet visits, you can also expect your dog to be checked and examined for worms. In this case, his vet will examine his stool.

Your first vet visit will also give you an idea of the vaccinations that he has to receive and when. As a guide, here are the usual vaccination schedules for miniature Goldendoodles:

- **6 weeks** – kennel cough and distemper, parainfluenza, and parvo vaccines. The breeder is often the one who takes care of this matter before he turns over the puppy to the new owner.

- **9 weeks** – kennel cough and distemper, parainfluenza, and parvo vaccine boosters

- **12 weeks** – leptospirosis and distemper, parainfluenza, and parvo vaccines

- **15 to 16 weeks** - leptospirosis and distemper, parainfluenza, and parvo vaccines, canine influenza vaccine, and rabies vaccine

Make sure that your miniature Goldendoodle receives all the vaccines he needs and at the right time. Aside from the vaccines, your puppy also needs tick, flea, and heartworm prevention. These parasites tend to cause some health issues in Goldendoodles. Some of these issues are even fatal, so you have to prevent them as much as possible by ensuring that your pet receives the required shots and visits his vet regularly.

Miniature Goldendoodle Diet

Your pet will also be at the pink of health if you make sure that he eats the right foods. The previous chapter already talked about the best foods that you can offer him. It would be best for you to stick to the recommendations as well as ensure that his diet consists of foods that can supply him with the nutrition he needs.

If you are still unsure what to do since you are a new fur parent, then you can always request a feeding chart from a reputable breeder. You can also talk to your vet to determine what you should feed your dog and how much.

One thing that you should avoid, though, is overeating as it may cause your pet to become overweight or obese. Make some adjustments to his diet if he becomes noticeably big. The good news is that cutting back or reducing his servings does not have to be gradual as you are allowed to do so right away.

However, if your goal is to make a transition to another kind of food, then it is advisable to do it slowly. Making abrupt changes from dry to raw foods or from commercial foods to a diet free of grain may only lead to stool and intestinal issues.

When it comes to changing foods, give your pet around ten to fourteen days to adjust. The new dog food also has to be introduced slowly and in small amounts. That way, he will not end up developing some health problems due to the sudden transition.

Miniature Goldendoodle Exercise and Activity Requirements

You can also maintain the excellent health of your miniature Goldendoodle by ensuring that he receives the right amount of exercise. Note that this breed is naturally active, so you have to give him some time to exercise and do a few activities daily. The reason behind the naturally active nature of the miniature Goldendoodle is that the two breeds where they came from – the Doodle and Golden Retriever – are also extremely active.

Basically, you need to give him thirty-minute walks twice a day and a weekly visit to the park. It is the standard requirement. However, some pet owners and breeders advise those who own Goldendoodles to give their pets three walks daily and around three to four park visits every week.

Every time you bring him outside, whether it is in the dog park or just the yard, you have to keep him on a leash. Note that the size of the miniature Goldendoodle may cause him to get darted beneath moving vehicles. If you let him run freely, then he is also prone to becoming prey to other pets and animals.

During puppyhood, try to avoid too rigorous exercises as much as possible. You can only give him more intense exercises once he is at least one year. You need to let him build up his stamina and strength first together with physical maturity.

To achieve that, you should divide his walks into easy parts while he is still a puppy. Make sure to include rest and relaxation time during this stage, too. Do that until he is already old enough and prepared to handle uninterrupted and long sessions physically.

If you are still unsure of how much exercise and activity he needs, do not be afraid to consult the breeder where you got him as well as your vet. As a basic guide, here are some exercises and activities that work well for miniature Goldendoodles:

- **Walking** – Walking is the most highly recommended exercise for miniature Goldendoodles. However, you have to make sure that you adjust the walking duration as well as the environment where he has to do it on his size.

- **Swimming** – It is a good activity for the miniature Goldendoodle considering the fact that both the parent breeds are attuned naturally to water.

- **Diving** – This is also a great activity for your miniature Goldendoodle, especially if there is a lake or pond nearby.

- **Agility play** – This one is also a fun and exciting activity for your miniature Goldendoodle. Just make sure to scale down the type and size of his toy depending on his current size.

The active nature of miniature Goldendoodles is the reason why you need to consider whether you have enough time for his exercises and activities before adopting this breed. Remember that inadequate exercise may lead him to display some unwanted behaviors, like digging, chewing, barking, and aggression. With that said, you need to give him the exercise he needs as this is also the key to keeping his weight and health in check. You can also use playtime for positive reinforcement and behavioral training.

Some Signs of Ailments to Watch Out For

When monitoring the health of your miniature Goldendoodle, you also have to be very keen and observant. This means you should watch out for any signs that he is ill, especially when he is still young. The reason is he is more prone to developing some ailments and diseases when he is still a puppy.

Some ailments are serious but most of them are actually one hundred percent preventable. You can prevent them by ensuring that your miniature Goldendoodle gets all his scheduled vaccines. However, even if your puppy is completely vaccinated, you should still watch out for these signs and contact his vet right away if he displays most, if not all, of them:

- Sudden loss of appetite, causing him to not eat at the appropriate times

- Inability to gain a healthy weight

- Painful and swollen stomach

- Vomiting

- Lethargy

- Diarrhea, accompanied with blood in the stool

- Coughing and some breathing difficulties

- Swollen and red eyes that may or may not come with discharge

- White gums

- Inability to poop or pee

- Nasal discharge

Most of these signs indicate that something is seriously wrong with your miniature Goldendoodle's health, so you have to contact his veterinarian right away. By doing that, you will immediately receive the best advice on how to handle the situation.

Possible Health Issues and Concerns

Each dog breed has its unique set of potential health issues and concerns. The same is true for miniature Goldendoodles. Yes, this breed is generally healthy but you can't still completely avoid some health concerns. Among the common health conditions that may affect miniature Goldendoodles are:

- **Patellar Luxation** – This health condition often occurs in small dog breeds. However, it may also develop in miniature Goldendoodles. It is characterized by the dog's knee joints slipping in and out of their proper place, leading to pain.

- **Hip dysplasia** – This health concern is usually hereditary. It happens once your dog's thighbone does not properly fit into the bone in his hips. It can eventually result in mobility issues and pain.

- **Elbow dysplasia** – It is also a degenerative disease, which can cause lameness or arthritis if left untreated in the long run. If your miniature Goldendoodle has this problem, then it is greatly possible that he will need medical attention. This will depend on how severe his case is.

- **Ear infections** – Note that one distinctive physical feature of miniature Goldendoodles is their floppy ears. The problem with it is that it can make your puppy more prone to trapping moisture. It can lead to infection if you do not check, monitor, and clean his ears frequently.

- **Hypothyroidism** – It refers to a thyroid gland disorder. Left untreated, it can lead to other issues on your dog's health, including skin disorders, obesity, epilepsy, and lethargy.

- **Progressive retinal atrophy** – This condition affects the eye of your dog. A sign of this condition is a slowly deteriorating retina that may result in blindness or loss of vision in the long run.

- **Allergies** – Similar to humans who have certain allergic reactions, dogs are prone to getting allergies, too. Some cases of allergic reactions you have to watch out for are contact, inhalant, and food allergies.

- **Von Willebrand's disease** – It refers to a blood condition, which significantly affects the process of forming blood clots. The good news is that this condition is curable. However, detailed treatments, as well as a surgical procedure, may be required.

If you notice your miniature Goldendoodle having signs of the mentioned diseases, visiting his veterinarian immediately is a must. You can also promote his optimum health and prevent the mentioned conditions by ensuring that he gets frequent medical exams. Give him proper care and attention, too, so his health will not be drastically affected.

Chapter 9

The Basics of Grooming

Learning how to groom your miniature Goldendoodle properly is also important. Note that this breed will most likely be at its happiest if you take care of everything. You have to set a routine for his exercise, training, playtime, as well as grooming. Make sure to train your dog to like the grooming routine, so he will look forward to it instead of avoiding it.

One important part of his grooming routine should be taking care of his coat. Whether he has the wooly and thick coat of the Poodle or the silky coat of the Golden Retriever, you need to make it a habit to groom it so he will be able to show its perfect version.

Caring for the Coat of Goldendoodle

Miniature Goldendoodles have different types of coats, including the straight one and the semi-wavy coat that also has a mixture of curly and straight locks. Regardless of the type of coat sported by your miniature Goldendoodle, you should still remember that grooming is a lifelong responsibility. With that said, you have to familiarize your pet with this routine while he is still young.

The amount of grooming needed by your pet will also greatly depend on the type of coat he has. You will know that he has the curly coat type even if he is still young if you notice some crimped hair on his ears, back, or forehead. If your puppy has a curly coat, then you have to brush it every day. The wavy or straight coat type, on the other hand, requires brushing once or twice every week.

Stick to the grooming and brushing required by your miniature Goldendoodle's coat as it is the key to preventing him from shedding. Some of those who own this breed make it a habit to clip the hair of their pets short, so grooming will be a lot easier. However, if you prefer to keep the hair of your pet long, then be prepared to commit to brushing it at least once every week.

Apart from regular brushing, the miniature Goldendoodle does not actually require too frequent baths. The reason is that this breed is capable of producing oils naturally, allowing them to retain the moisture and smoothness of their coats. You only need to bathe him when extremely necessary, usually once every 3 to 4 weeks. However, you may have to increase that frequency if your pet is extremely active outdoors.

If his fur gets tangled and matted too frequently, then you may need to buy a sturdy slicker brush, which works in releasing his collected hair by just pressing a button. One advantage of this brush is that you can use it every day. It also works well when it comes to distributing the natural oils coming from the skin throughout his coat, keeping it soft, smooth, and properly moisturized. In addition, the brush is a big help in getting rid of debris and dander that may have been trapped within the coat.

Another great thing that you can use is a coat spray specifically designed for pre-brushing. You may have to spend more for this product but it is worth investing in as it promotes ease in dematting your dog's fur or coat while retaining its silky and soft texture. If you have no plans to spend more on a coat spray, then a dematting comb will already do you a good favor.

It can target the undercoat, which is somewhat thick and hard to reach. What is great about this comb is that it is designed in such a way that it can target your dog's undercoat using just a gentle and soft touch. It is a good thing, especially if you do not want him to get hurt every time you groom him and try to make his coat well-kept and pleasant-looking.

Another product that you can use to prevent tangles and mats from forming on his hair and coat is a detangler and/or light conditioner. It would be best to put on this product after shampooing your pet. It serves as a preventive measure for tangles. Make it a point to brush his coat thoroughly before giving him a bath. The reason is that once the mats or tangles get wet, you will have a difficult time removing them.

Basics of Bathing

As mentioned earlier, the miniature Goldendoodle does not require too frequent bathing. With that said, you have full discretion as to how frequently you will be bathing him. Some of those who own this breed make it a habit to bathe their dogs one or two times per month. You can choose to drop him off at a groomer, so you won't have to do all the hard work.

However, if you want to do it on your own, then you should decide on the bathing frequency depending on his habits. For instance, if he spends a lot of time outdoors, plays with you and other pets too often, swim or do other tiring activities, then you may need to increase the frequency of bathing. This is important in removing the stink, debris, and dirt that may have accumulated on his skin and fur. Note that if left uncleaned, the buildup may lead to allergies and irritations.

When bathing your miniature Goldendoodle, it would be best to use a hypoallergenic and gentle shampoo even if this breed is known for not having overly sensitive skin. If possible, go for all-natural bathing products, including shampoo, so you will have one hundred percent assurance that they are safe and gentle for your dog.

Bathing your miniature Goldendoodle also requires you to use a washcloth and lukewarm water – the only things you need to lather him up. After that, you need to rinse him thoroughly. If possible, do the rinsing twice to ensure that no residue and dirt remain on his skin.

You should follow up the bathing with the application of a light conditioner and detangler. If possible, use a silicone detangler, which can provide lightweight moisture to his coat, making it naturally fluffy.

Another tip is to dry his coat completely before you clip or trim his coat.

The good thing about bathing him and keeping his coat clean and in good condition is that it allows you to spot bumps, lumps, or any other problems on his skin. Use this time to examine his skin, so you can catch any issue right away. The time you spend grooming is also good for him as it can massage his skin, thereby promoting better health and blood circulation. Moreover, it sorts of make you bond with him. Note that your dog loves it when you care for him, so grooming is something that he will look forward to.

Other Parts of your Pet that Require Grooming and Maintenance

Apart from the coat, there are also other parts of your miniature Goldendoodle that require regular grooming and maintenance. Among those you should focus on are the following:

Teeth

One important aspect of taking care of your miniature Goldendoodle is his dental health. When taking care of his dental health, you have to know the usual time through which this breed loses its teeth. In most cases, a Goldendoodle puppy has sharp teeth, referred to as milk teeth, that begin to lose or fall out at around eight to ten weeks. You can then expect these lost teeth to be replaced by permanent ones once he reaches three to four months.

Once your miniature Goldendoodle already has permanent teeth, make sure to make it a habit to brush them twice or thrice weekly. This is a vital routine as it can help in preventing plaque and tartar from accumulating on his teeth. Regular brushing is also crucial in preventing your Goldendoodle from having bad breath.

You can brush his teeth using a regular toothbrush. However, you have to pair it up with canine toothpaste. This toothpaste is the safest one for dogs as the one that humans use can cause him to get sick if he accidentally swallows it.

Ears

You also have to take care of your miniature Goldendoodle's ears. You can do that by cleaning his ears periodically or regularly. Remember that your dog is prone to collecting debris and dirt on his ears that may even lead to infection.

If you do not clean his ears regularly and the buildup is already too much, then he will be at risk of dealing with hair loss. To prevent that problem, make it a habit to clean his ears once every month at the very least. In this case, you should use a canine ear cleaning solution, which you can often buy online and from pet stores.

Check the instructions stated on the label regarding its use. Also, make sure that you have cotton balls around. It would be better to use these cotton balls in wiping and removing excess solution from the area instead of those with Q-tips. The reason is that such cotton balls are gentler and safer on his ears.

Nails

Make sure that his nails are also given proper attention. Observe his nails so you will know when is the perfect time to give them a trim. One sign that indicates it is time to trim is when his nails start clicking on hard and tough surfaces. The best tool that you can use for nail trimming is a standard clipper. You can use it in cutting his nails close to his toes.

Be extra careful and avoid cutting the quick, which refers to the blood vessel that runs through the nail. The reason is that it may cause his nails to bleed. In worse cases, it can cause some pain that may be traumatic for him. If he experiences that, then there is a great chance that he will fear the next time you trim his nails, making it quite hard to establish this grooming routine.

Preventing Fleas and Ticks

One problem that your miniature Goldendoodle may encounter is the presence of mites, ticks, and fleas, among many other pests, in his ears. The best way to prevent them is to visit a veterinarian, but there are also some tips and tricks you can apply to prevent and treat the pests. Here are just some preventive measures:

- **Use a flea collar** – Put it on your dog to prevent pests from invading. If possible, use a flea comb when brushing his coat and hair once weekly.

- **Spend time examining his ears** – Make it a habit to do a regular examination of his ears to see signs of the pests. Among those that you should watch out for are small black dots. The presence of these dots indicates that there are fleas or mites on his ears.

- **Wash and clean his beddings regularly** – Do it at least once every week.

- **Clean the lawn regularly** – Ensure that it is devoid of leaf piles and yard clippings as pets tend to thrive in areas with moist vegetation.

For severe cases, you should always see your miniature Goldendoodle's veterinarian. Make it a point to use sprays, shampoos, and powders, too. If the case is really extreme, then you may need to use an indoor fogger or spray to exterminate the pests. You may also want to apply lawn treatments to free your place of them and prevent them from invading any part of your miniature Goldendoodle's body.

Conclusion

Dogs are among the most amazing pets that you can own. They even serve as man's best friend. You can especially prove that saying by choosing to own a miniature Goldendoodle as your pet. The reason is that they have all the nice qualities that make them truly great companions.

However, just like other pets, it is necessary to arm yourself with the right amount of knowledge on how to take care of them. You can't just bring one home without doing all the necessary preparations. You need to be aware of how you can take care of them and prepare your home for his arrival.

Also, you need to commit to spending quality time with him. Hopefully, the contents of this book will guide you all throughout that process. In the end, you should be able to use it as your go-to guide in learning everything that you need to know about miniature Goldendoodles and how you can give them the care and attention they need.

Made in the USA
Monee, IL
17 September 2021